Marian Pickman

New Yorkie Dog

www.olympiapublishers.com
OLYMPIA PAPERBACK EDITION

Copyright © Marian Pickman 2024

The right of Marian Pickman to be identified as author of this work has been asserted in accordance with sections 77 and 78 of the Copyright, Designs and Patents Act 1988.

All Rights Reserved

No reproduction, copy or transmission of this publication may be made without written permission.
No paragraph of this publication may be reproduced, copied or transmitted save with the written permission of the publisher, or in accordance with the provisions of the Copyright Act 1956 (as amended).

Any person who commits any unauthorised act in relation to this publication may be liable to criminal prosecution and civil claims for damage.

A CIP catalogue record for this title is available from the British Library.

ISBN: 978-1-80439-551-6

This is a work of fiction.
Names, characters, places and incidents originate from the writer's imagination. Any resemblance to actual persons, living or dead, is purely coincidental.

First Published in 2024

Olympia Publishers
Tallis House
2 Tallis Street
London
EC4Y 0AB

Printed in Great Britain

Dedication

I dedicate this book with love to my husband Evan and my children and grandchildren who have been my critics and coaches, encouraging and appreciating my efforts.

Welcome to the Big Appuli, home of the .....

Statue of Laberty

Empoodle State Building

United Dalmations

Central Peek

Pawberry Fields

Walk along Bark Avenue

Ride the NYC Pugway

Visit Greyhound Central Terminal

Chowna Town

Greenwich Vizsla

St.Pappillion's Cathedral

or Central Chinagogue

Be Sure to See Rottiefeller Center

Collieumbia University

And Welsh Street

Walk the High Line and
Explore Pupson Yards

Take a Tour of NBC Shih Tzudios

See the Night Lights on the George Weimaraner Bridge

And Gracie Mastiff

And don't forget the
NY Public Labradoodle.

Sports fans will want to visit Malamute Square Garden,

home of the

Rangers and Knickerboxers

Play at Shelty Piers

Or maybe you will catch
the NYC Marabichon!

Or the Macy's
Thanksgiving Dane Parade

Pay your respects at Hound Zero

Ride the Staten Island Furry

or the tram to Roosevelt Highland

Take in a show on Briardway,

or Lincoln Setter

Radio Scotty Music Hall

or the Muttropolitan Opera

Enjoy the New York Philharmongrel

The NYC Bullet

And how do you get to Cairnegie Hall?
Pracrice practice practice

Shop at Bloomairedales

Sacks Spitz avenue

And Birddog Goodman

Don't miss the
Museum of Natchihuahua History

The Hayden Planeterrierum,

The Metropomeranian Museum of Art

The Museum of Modern Arf

Solomon Goldenheim Museum

Or the murals on the Bowwowery

And for a snack don't miss a NY staple, a Beagle and Lox!

Now that you have completed your tour, we would like to present you with Akita the City.

About the Author

I have been a free-lance artist since graduating from Pratt Institute in New York as an advertising and illustration major. I have worked for various companies designing greeting cards, logos, and gift and display items, as well as painting custom portraits and murals. I have illustrated many books and children's books for other authors, and am now thrilled to do one of my own. I have tried to combine my sense of humor and my love of dogs into a whimsical fun tour of the city I love.

Acknowledgements

Thank you to my closest friends, Jayne, Andi and Cheryl who allow me to bounce ideas off of them, and to Marc Bloom for his publishing advice. I want to thank my beautiful Border Collie Scout up in dog heaven for inspiring me and loving me unconditionally.